Copyright © 2018 by Learning with Harmony, LLC.
www.learningwithharmony.com
Book Cover & Illustrations Designed by Aranahaj Iqbal

All rights reserved. No part of this book may be reproduced or transmitted in any form or by any means, electronic or mechanical, including photocopying, recording, or by any information storage and retrieval system, without permission in writing from the author.

ISBN-13: 978-1-948398-05-3

About the Author

LaTonya D. Steele has spent 20+ years of her career teaching high school and adult learners business courses in the community college system. She is a firm believer that a good education is essential for all ages. She has a passion for giving back to others and helping them succeed in reaching their academic, professional and personal goals. LaTonya has a Ph.D. in Management and is a lifelong learner.

Since the birth of her first granddaughter, LaTonya has recently developed a new interest in writing educational books for children. She started writing books for her granddaughter and wanted to share them with other children, families, caregivers, and early childhood educators. LaTonya decided to make an educational book series (**Learning with Harmony**) for children from birth to 4 years old. The main characters in the book are her granddaughter Harmony and dog Penny. You can visit her website at www.learningwithharmony.com.

About the Illustrator

Aranahaj Iqbal has been illustrating for over 5 years and has many published books. She enjoys illustrating children's books. She also provides illustrations for book series, single books, and long-term projects. You can visit her Facebook page at facebook.com/aranahajart, Instagram at aranahajiqbal and Twitter at Aranahaji (ARANAHAHJI) to see her portfolios.

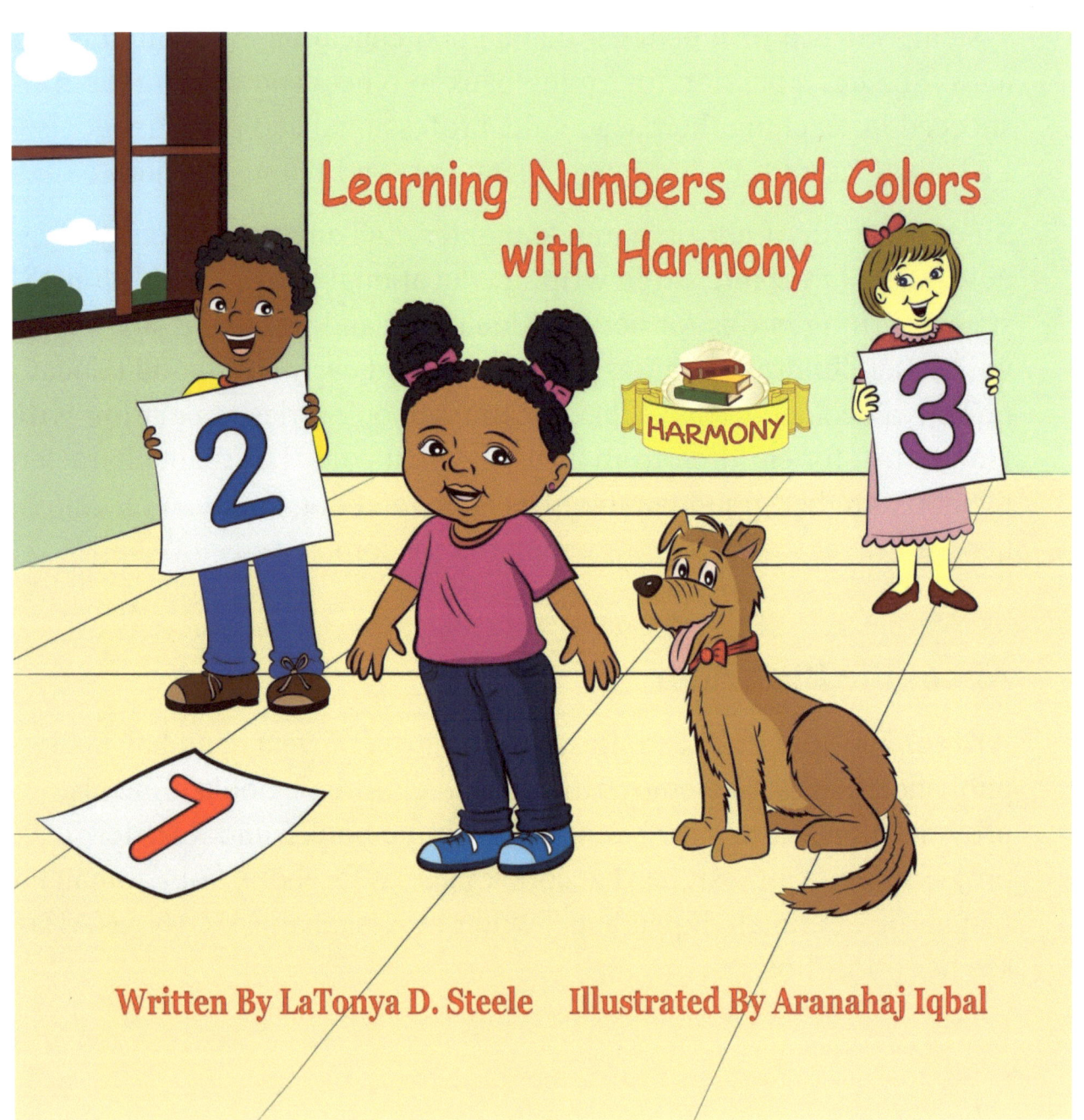

1

One orange sun.

Hi! My name is Harmony. I like to have fun under the orange sun.

Count the orange sun with me in the sky.

one

2

Two blue shoes.

Do you like my new blue shoes?

Help me count the blue shoes on my feet.

one   two

3

Three green trees.

Do you like to play near the green trees in the backyard?

How many green trees do you see in my backyard?

one   two   three

4

Four red doors.

My dog Penny and I like to sit on the floor near the red doors.

Count the red doors with me.

one two three four

5

Five gray beehives.

Can you see the bees flying near the gray beehives?

How many gray beehives are on the tree branch?

one two three four five

6

Six yellow chicks.

Penny likes to chase the yellow chicks.

Count the yellow chicks with me.

one two three four five six

7

Seven black ravens.

I like to watch the black ravens fly in the sky.

How many black ravens are flying in the sky?

one   two   three   four   five   six   seven

8

Eight white plates.

What is your favorite food to put on white plates?

Count the white plates on the table with me.

one two three four five six seven eight

9

Nine pink signs.

My mom put the pink signs on the wall in my room.

How many pink signs are hanging on the wall?

one   two   three   four   five   six   seven   eight   nine

10

Ten brown hens.

The brown hens are ready to lay eggs soon.

How many brown hens do you see?

one two three four five six seven eight nine ten

Learning is so much fun! Let's practice reading the numbers and colors together now.

One

Orange

Two

Blue

Three
Green

Four

Red

Five

Gray

Six

Yellow

Seven

Black

Eight

White

Nine

Pink

Ten

Brown

www.ingramcontent.com/pod-product-compliance
Lightning Source LLC
Chambersburg PA
CBHW041226040426
42444CB00002B/69